STAR WARS™

GALACTIC BAKING

GALACTIC BAKING

THE OFFICIAL COOKBOOK OF SWEET AND SAVORY
TREATS FROM TATOOINE, HOTH, AND BEYOND

INSIGHT
EDITIONS

San Rafael • Los Angeles • London

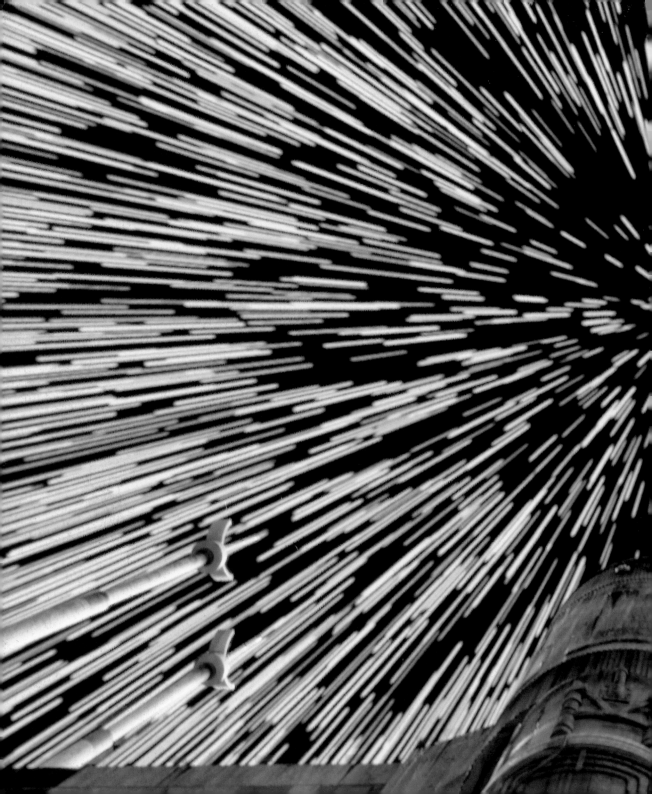

CONTENTS

INTRODUCTION

NO MATTER HOW YOU TRAVEL THROUGH THE GALAXY—IN AN X-WING, A STAR Destroyer, or a speeder—the best way to experience a new place is through food.

The recipes in this book provide fun and family-friendly baked goods inspired by the worlds of *Star Wars*. You will travel to the desert planets of Tatooine, Jakku, and Pasaana; the snow-covered worlds of Hoth and Starkiller Base; the lush expanses of Endor, Naboo, Ahch-To, and Ajan Kloss; space stations and metropolises like Cloud City; and even the inhospitable regions of Dagobah and Mustafar.

Bake a batch of Bantha Blue Butter Sandwich Cookies (page 14) for a birthday party. Make Podrace Puffs (page 36) or Puffer Pig Pocket Pizzas (page 79) for a sleepover or movie night at home. Embrace the power of the dark side with Sith Cookies (page 35) or impress your friends with a chocolaty Forest of Endor Log Cake (page 64). Whether you're a Padawan or a Jedi Master in the kitchen, you'll find something to inspire you and take you on a journey to a galaxy far, far away.

A few things you should know before you embark: Some of the recipes have one of the following symbols:

 LIGHTSPEED RECIPE

This means the prep time for the recipe is just about 30 minutes or less.

 DARK-SIDE RECIPE

These are particularly rich and indulgent treats.

 LIGHT-SIDE RECIPE

These are on the healthier side, whether from the addition of whole grains or because they have less sugar, calories, and fat than some of the other recipes.

So get out your mudhorn eggs and blue milk, and get baking. May the Force—and flour—be with you!

BAKING TOOLS

BAKING SHEETS, especially thick, heavy ones, help cookies bake evenly.

COOKIE CUTTERS come in lots of shapes—even *Star Wars* characters (page 58)—but a set of round cutters in different sizes is essential.

SMALL METAL ICING SPATULAS, both straight and angled offset ones, make spreading frosting on cupcakes and cakes easy.

A **PIPING BAG** fitted with a **PASTRY TIP** is a must for decorating all kinds of baked goods. Pastry tips come in lots of different shapes, but plain tips in different sizes are the best ones to have for this book.

OVEN MITTS or pads protect hands from hot pans, oven racks, baking dishes, and hot lava!

PARCHMENT PAPER prevents baked goods from sticking to pans and makes clean up easier, too. If you don't have parchment, you can use vegetable oil, butter and a dusting of flour, or nonstick baking spray.

A **HAND MIXER** makes quick work of blending batters and frostings, beating egg whites and cream, and more. You can use a mixing bowl and wooden spoon or whisk—and your baking muscles!—instead.

A **RUBBER SPATULA** is handy for folding ingredients together and scraping batters into pans.

A **SPRINGFORM PAN** has a clasp that lets you loosen and remove the pan sides after baking.

DESERT WORLDS

From the junkyards of Jakku to the streets of Mos Espa
and the bleached dunes of Pasaana, these treats make
life on the sandiest planets in the galaxy a little bit sweeter.

BANTHA BLUE BUTTER SANDWICH COOKIES

When a bantha gives blue milk, you get blue butter. These rich cookies are filled with ice cream to make a two-in-one treat. Enjoy with a glass of blue milk, if you like.

ACTIVE TIME 45 MIN   TOTAL TIME 1 HR 25 MIN   MAKES ABOUT 20 SANDWICH COOKIES

2¾ cups all-purpose flour

1 teaspoon baking soda

½ teaspoon baking powder

1 cup unsalted butter, softened

1½ cups granulated sugar

1 large egg

1 teaspoon vanilla extract

1 teaspoon blue food coloring gel

Rainbow sprinkles

1 quart vanilla or birthday cake–flavored ice cream

1. Preheat oven to 375°F. In a medium bowl stir together flour, baking soda, and baking powder. In a large mixing bowl beat butter with a hand mixer until softened. Gradually beat in sugar until light and fluffy. Beat in egg, vanilla, and food coloring. Gradually add flour mixture and beat until combined.

2. Line two large rimmed baking sheets with parchment paper. Place rounded tablespoonfuls of dough 2 inches apart on prepared baking sheets. Bake for 8 to 10 minutes or just until done in center and edges are barely browned. Let cool on baking sheets for 5 minutes. Transfer cookies to a cooling rack to cool completely. When cooled, chill cookies in the freezer for about 30 minutes before filling.

3. Place sprinkles in a shallow bowl and put in freezer to chill. Allow ice cream to soften at room temperature for 10 minutes before filling cookies.

4. To fill cookies, place a small scoop of ice cream on bottom side of a chilled cookie. Top with another cookie. Press together until ice cream is squished to edges of cookies. Quickly roll edges in chilled sprinkles and place cookie sandwich in a container in the freezer. Repeat with remaining cookies, ice cream, and sprinkles.

JAKKU JUNKYARD TREATS

Cobbling together junk and scraps is just part of life as a scavenger in the Jakku desert. Coated in a sweet and slightly spicy pumpkin-spiced glaze and baked until crunchy, this seemingly random assortment of ingredients comes together to create an awesome snack.

ACTIVE TIME 5 MIN   TOTAL TIME 30 MIN   MAKES ABOUT 9 CUPS

- 1 cup pretzel sticks
- 1½ cups O-shape cereal
- 1½ cups square checkerboard cereal
- 1½ cups bugle-shape snack chips
- 2 cups broken saltine crackers (large pieces)
- ¾ cup honey
- 3 tablespoons canola oil
- 2 teaspoons pumpkin pie spice
- ⅛ to ¼ teaspoon cayenne pepper
- 1 cup snipped dried fruit (apricots, cranberries, raisins)
- ½ cup pumpkin seeds or peanuts

1. Preheat oven to 300°F. Grease a large rimmed baking sheet. Place pretzel sticks, cereals, bugle chips, and saltines on the pan; stir to mix.

2. In a medium saucepan combine honey, oil, pumpkin pie spice, and cayenne. Cook and stir over medium heat just until hot and edges begin to bubble. Set aside.

3. Bake cereal mixture for 5 minutes. Pour hot honey mixture over warm cereal and stir to coat. Return to oven for 20 to 25 minutes more or until mixture begins to brown, stirring after 10 minutes. Remove from oven and immediately stir in dried fruit and pumpkin seeds. Spread hot mixture out onto a large piece of greased foil. Cool completely. When cool, break mixture into chunks.

4. Store in an airtight container at room temperature.

TATOOINE SANDIES

Young Anakin would like this type of sandie—a cookie with rich flavor and a crumbly, fine texture from the combination of butter and chopped nuts. He might have a hard time choosing between white and dark chocolate, but you don't have to.

ACTIVE TIME 45 MIN   TOTAL TIME 1 HR 20 MIN   MAKES 18 COOKIES

2 cups all-purpose flour

1 cup pecans, coarsely chopped

¾ cup salted butter, room temperature

¾ cup powdered sugar

1 tablespoon milk

¼ teaspoon salt

1 teaspoon vanilla

½ cup coarse sugar

1 cup white chocolate chips

4 teaspoons vegetable shortening, divided

1 cup semisweet chocolate chips

1. Preheat oven to 350°F. Line two large rimmed baking sheets with parchment paper. in a medium bowl toss together flour and pecans; set aside.

2. In a large bowl, beat butter at with a hand mixer at medium-low speed until smooth. Add powdered sugar, milk, salt, and vanilla; beat 2 minutes or until fluffy, stopping to scrape bowl as needed. Add the flour mixture, and beat at low speed 30 seconds or just until combined.

3. Shape dough into 2-inch balls and roll in coarse sugar. Place 1 ½ inches apart on prepared pans. With the bottom of a glass, lightly flatten each ball into a ¼-inch-thick disk.

4. Bake 15 to 17 minutes until cookies are golden brown, rotating sheets halfway through. Remove from oven and cool on pan for 5 minutes. Transfer cookies to cooling racks and cool completely.

5. Meanwhile, place the white chocolate chips and 2 teaspoons of the shortening in a microwave-safe bowl and microwave on 50 percent power for 60 seconds. Stir well and then heat for 20-second increments on 50 percent until the chocolate is nearly melted, stirring after each interval. Dip one side of the cookies into the white chocolate and place dipped-side up onto a cooling rack to firm up chocolate. Repeat microwave and dipping process with semisweet chocolate chips, remaining shortening, and remaining cookies to form a "V" shape between the two chocolate dips.

CHANCE CUBE CAKES

Carried by the likes of Han Solo and Watto, chance cubes belong to those looking to test their luck. However, there's always a good outcome when you make these tasty wagering dice. Starting with frozen pound cakes makes the process even easier.

ACTIVE TIME 1 HR 15 MIN   TOTAL TIME 2 HRS 15 MIN   MAKES 9 CAKE CUBES

EASY MARSHMALLOW FONDANT

- 8 ounces mini marshmallows
- 2 tablespoons water
- 1 tablespoon unsalted butter
- 2½ cups sifted powdered sugar, divided, plus more for dusting if needed

CAKE CUBES

- 3 (10.75-ounce) purchased frozen pound cakes, thawed
- 1 cup canned vanilla frosting

FOOD COLOR PAINT

- ¼ teaspoon each red and blue gel food coloring
- 2 to 4 teaspoons vodka

1. **For Easy Marshmallow Fondant:** Combine marshmallows, the water, and butter in a large microwave-safe bowl. Microwave on high for about 1 minute or until marshmallows and butter are melted. Stir to combine well. Stir in 2 cups of the powdered sugar with a wooden spoon. Scrape from bowl and mound onto plastic wrap. Wrap fondant and allow to cool for a few hours or overnight. (Or chill for 1 hour until firm.) When ready to use, remove plastic wrap and place on a surface dusted with more sifted powdered sugar. Knead in up to ½ cup of additional sifted powdered sugar until no longer sticky.

2. To make cakes, pinch off nine walnut-size pieces of fondant. Dust a work surface with powdered sugar. Use a rolling pin to roll out fondant balls to ¼-inch thickness, about 6 inches in diameter. If fondant becomes sticky when rolling, dust with more powdered sugar.

3. **For Cake Cubes:** Using a sharp knife, trim tops and sides of each cake. Cut each pound cake into three 2-inch cubes. Frost tops and sides with a thin layer of vanilla frosting. Drape a fondant disk over the top of a frosted cake cube. Press fondant to sides of cake, allowing excess to pinch together at corners. Use kitchen shears to trim away excess fondant at corners. Smooth corners if desired. Trim excess fondant away at bottom edges. Repeat with remaining cake cubes. Cake cubes are now ready to paint. Wrap remaining fondant with plastic wrap and store in refrigerator for another use.

continued on page 23

continued from page 20

4. **For Food Color Paint:** Place red and blue gel food coloring in two tiny bowls. Stir 1 to 2 teaspoons vodka into each bowl.

5. Using a clean artists brush, lightly brush three sides of a cake cube with the red paint. (Paint a square area of color on each cake side and brush lightly so that paint doesn't cover all of cake sides—you want some fondant to show through). Using another clean artists brush, lightly brush the two remaining fondant-covered sides of the cube with the blue paint. On a second cake cube, brush three sides of the cube with blue paint and the two remaining fondant-covered sides of the cube with the red paint. Repeat sequence with remaining cake cubes.

RANCOR CLAWS

Contrary to popular belief, rancors are often harmless when found in the wild and are only driven to hostility by cruel owners like Jabba the Hutt. These claws—fashioned from flaky pastry and an almond-chocolate-hazelnut filling—are a tribute to the sweet, if short-lived, relationship between Jabba's rancor, Pateesa, and creature caretaker Malakili.

ACTIVE TIME 30 MIN TOTAL TIME 55 MIN MAKES 8 PASTRIES

⅓ cup almond paste
1 cup ground almonds
¼ cup granulated sugar
3 tablespoons chocolate-hazelnut spread
1 egg white
½ teaspoon almond extract
All-purpose flour
1 (17.3-ounce) box frozen puff pastry, thawed (2 sheets)
1 egg
1 tablespoon water
Coarse sugar
Sliced almonds

1. Preheat oven to 400°F. Line two large rimmed baking sheets with parchment paper. In a mixing bowl beat almond paste with a hand mixer to crumble. Add the ground almonds and granulated sugar; beat until well combined. Add hazelnut spread, egg white, and almond extract. Beat on low speed for 30 seconds to combine. Beat on high speed until fluffy, about 3 minutes. Set aside. In a small bowl beat together the whole egg and water. Set aside.

2. Lightly dust a work surface with flour. Unfold one sheet of puff pastry and lightly roll out to a 12×12-inch square. Cut pastry into four 6-inch squares. Spoon about 1 tablespoon filling in a stripe down center of each square. Lightly brush edges of pastry with egg wash. Fold squares in half over the filling. Press edges together to seal. Transfer to prepared baking sheet. Repeat with other sheet of dough and remaining filling. To make claws, cut four 1-inch slits into the long, sealed edge of each pastry. Fan the pastry slightly to separate the "claws." Brush tops of pastry with egg wash and sprinkle with coarse sugar. Lightly press an almond slice into the end of each claw.

3. Bake 25 to 30 minutes, or until puffed and light brown. Cool on a wire rack.

BB-8 CAKES

In the words of Leia Organa, "never underestimate a droid"—or these treats, which will surely appeal to all ages and tastes!

ACTIVE TIME 2 HRS   TOTAL TIME 2 HRS 45 MIN   MAKES 12 CUPCAKES

1 ½ cups all-purpose flour

⅔ cup granulated sugar

2 teaspoons baking powder

⅔ cup whole milk

¼ cup unsalted butter, very soft

1 large egg

1 teaspoon vanilla extract

1 (16-ounce) can vanilla frosting, divided

12 plain donut holes

Orange and black gel food coloring

Black or brown mini and regular-size round candy-coated chocolate pieces and silver dragees

1. Preheat oven to 350°F. Line a cupcake pan with 12 paper or foil liners. In a medium mixing bowl combine flour, sugar, and baking powder. Add milk, butter, egg, and vanilla. Beat with a hand mixer on low speed until combined. Beat on medium speed for 1 minute. Divide batter among cupcake liners in pan (two-thirds full to ensure rounded tops after baking). Bake about 15 minutes or until a toothpick inserted comes out clean. Cool on a wire rack.

2. Place about 1 cup of canned frosting in a small microwave-safe bowl. Microwave on high for 15 seconds, then stir. Continue to microwave and stir, 10 seconds at a time, until frosting is just soft enough to pour from a spoon. Dip tops of cupcakes into the soft frosting and return to cooling rack. With a sharp knife, remove a ¼-inch slice from bottom of each donut hole. If necessary, reheat frosting to keep it spoonable. With a fork, hold a donut hole over bowl of softened frosting. Spoon frosting over donut hole to cover. Carefully place the frosted donut hole on top of a frosted cupcake. Chill cupcakes a few minutes to set frosting.

3. Divide remaining unmelted frosting between two small bowls. Tint one portion orange and the other portion gray. Place colored frosting in disposable decorating bags. Snip tips of bags to make very small openings. Decorate cupcakes with colored frosting, making stripes, circles, and dots. Add candy-coated chocolate pieces and silver dragees.

FESTIVAL OF THE ANCESTORS COOKIES

The jewel-tone centers of these buttery cookies—made with crushed and melted hard candies—celebrate the color, clothing, and kites of the Aki-Aki and their Festival of the Ancestors in the desert of Pasaana. Though this celebration only occurs once every 42 years, these colorful cookies can be enjoyed at any time!

ACTIVE TIME 1 HR   TOTAL TIME 1 HR 10 MIN   MAKES 2 DOZEN COOKIES

2¾ cups all-purpose flour
½ teaspoon baking powder
½ teaspoon baking soda
½ teaspoon salt
1 cup unsalted butter, room temperature
½ cup granulated sugar
½ cup light corn syrup
½ teaspoon almond extract
1 (14-ounce) package fruit-flavor rectangular hard candies (watermelon, green apple, cherry, grape, blue raspberry)

1. Preheat oven to 350°F and line two large rimmed baking sheets with foil.

2. In a medium bowl mix the flour, baking powder, baking soda, and salt. In a separate large bowl beat the butter and sugar with a hand mixer until light and fluffy. Beat in corn syrup and almond extract. On low speed, beat in the flour mixture. Divide dough in half; shape into disks and wrap in plastic wrap. Refrigerate 20 minutes.

3. Meanwhile, unwrap and sort candies by color. Place candies in small freezer bags. Use a mallet to coarsely crush candy.

4. Place one disk of dough between two sheets of waxed paper or parchment paper. Roll evenly to ¼-inch thickness. Remove the top sheet of paper. Using a 3-inch round cutter, cut dough into circles. Using a 2-inch cutter, cut out the center of each circle to create a ring. Remove center dough and reserve scraps to roll out additional cookies. Using a flat spatula, gently transfer shaped dough to the prepared baking sheets. Repeat with remaining dough.

continued on page 31

continued from page 28

5. Using a small spoon, fill each cutout hole with one or more colors of the pulverized candies—do not overflow edges.

6. Bake for 8 to 10 minutes or until cookies are golden and candy just melts. Remove the baking sheets from oven and place on a rack to cool. (Do not remove cookies, as candy has to harden.) When cool, gently peel away foil.

   TO STORE: Store cookies, layered between waxed paper, in airtight containers.

MOS EISLEY CANTINA MUNCHIES

When you're tossing back beverages in this "wretched hive of scum and villainy," you need something to chomp on. These delicious munchies—thanks to a tasty mix of salty, sweet, and spicy ingredients—provide just that.

ACTIVE TIME 5 MIN   TOTAL TIME 35 MIN   MAKES ABOUT 18 (½-CUP) SERVINGS

2 tablespoons sriracha hot sauce

2 tablespoons honey

2 tablespoons butter, melted

2 teaspoons soy sauce

2 cups hexagon-shape corn and rice cereal

2 cups pretzel nuggets

2 cups cheese balls

2 beef jerky sticks, cut into ½-inch pieces

1 cup goldfish-shape cheese crackers

½ cup smoked almonds

Kosher salt

1. Heat oven to 300°F. Line a large rimmed baking sheet with parchment paper; set aside. In a large bowl combine sriracha, honey, butter, and soy sauce. Whisk to combine.

2. Add cereal, pretzel nuggets, cheese balls, jerky, crackers, and almonds. Mix well to completely coat with the sriracha-honey sauce.

3. Spread mixture on the prepared pan and sprinkle lightly with salt. Bake for 30 minutes, stirring every 10 minutes. Remove from oven and let cool completely.

4. Store in an airtight container at room temperature.

SITH COOKIES

Wondering what dark-side techniques are behind these cookies? A coating of cocoa powder wicks some of the surface moisture from the dough balls as the cookies bake, creating cracks in the surface to reveal the red velvet interior. Perfect for taking with you on a journey to the Sith Citadel of the dark, desolate planet Exegol.

ACTIVE TIME 45 MIN   TOTAL TIME 3 HRS   MAKES 30 COOKIES

- 3 cups all-purpose flour
- 1 cup + 1 tablespoon unsweetened dark cocoa powder, divided
- 2 teaspoons baking powder
- ¼ teaspoon baking soda
- ¾ teaspoon salt
- ¾ cup unsalted butter, softened
- 1⅓ cups granulated sugar
- 3 large eggs
- 1 tablespoon whole milk
- 1½ teaspoons vanilla extract
- 2 teaspoons lemon juice
- 1 (1-ounce) bottle red food coloring

1. Preheat oven to 350°F.

2. In a mixing bowl whisk together flour, the 1 tablespoon cocoa powder, the baking powder, baking soda, and salt; set aside.

3. In the bowl of a stand mixer fitted with the paddle attachment, whip butter and granulated sugar until pale and fluffy. Mix in eggs one at a time, blending until combined after each addition. Mix in milk, vanilla, lemon juice, and red food coloring. Mix in flour mixture on low speed just until combined. Cover bowl with plastic wrap and chill 2 hours or until firm enough to shape into balls.

4. Line two large rimmed baking sheets with parchment paper. Place the remaining 1 cup cocoa powder in a shallow dish. Remove dough from refrigerator and shape into 1-inch balls. Roll each cookie ball into cocoa powder and evenly coat. Transfer to prepared pans, spacing 1½ inches apart. Bake the cookies for 8 to 10 minutes. Remove from the oven when the cookies are just set on the edges, but before they get too browned.

5. Let cool on the pan 5 minutes. Transfer to a wire rack to cool completely.

   TO STORE: Store at room temperature in an airtight container. (You can also freeze them in layers, placing parchment paper between layers so the cookies don't stick when you thaw them.)

PODRACE PUFFS

Hit the concession stand at the track for a bag of these cheesy,
pepperoni-topped puffs before heading to the stands to cheer
on your favorite racer. Eat 'em while they're hot!

ACTIVE TIME 10 MIN   TOTAL TIME 30 MIN   MAKES 24 PUFFS

1 cup whole milk

2 large eggs

1 cup all-purpose flour

2 tablespoons butter,
melted, divided

½ teaspoon salt

⅛ teaspoon black pepper

2 teaspoons dried pizza
seasoning

24 pepperoni minis

1 tablespoon finely grated
Parmesan cheese, divided

1. In a medium bowl whisk together milk, eggs, flour,
1 tablespoon of the butter, the salt, and pepper until smooth.
Stir in pizza seasoning.

2. Preheat oven to 425°F with a rack in upper third of the
oven. Butter a 24-cup mini-muffin pan with the remaining
1 tablespoon butter. Place the pan in the oven until the butter
sizzles, about 2 minutes.

3. Gently stir batter, then divide among muffin cups (they will be
about two-thirds full). Top each puff with a slice of pepperoni.
Sprinkle with half of the Parmesan. Bake 18 to 20 minutes or
until puffed and golden brown.

4. Remove from oven and sprinkle each puff with remaining
Parmesan cheese. Serve immediately.

MOS EISLEY CANTINA CUPCAKES

The glowing drinks and good music at this Tatooine watering hole draw a diverse crowd of pilots, smugglers, bounty hunters, and general misfits and renegades. Re-create a few of the regulars with your favorite cupcakes and just a few simple ingredients.

Baked cupcakes

Creamy decorator icing (not canned icing)

Paste or gel food coloring (black, green, peach or orange, and yellow)

Cotton candy

Brown mini round candy-coated chocolate pieces

Pretzel sticks

Round black candies

Black licorice

MUFTAK

THIS FURRY PICKPOCKET FREQUENTS THE CANTINA TO STAY COOL IN THE TATOOINE HEAT. HE MAY HAVE FOUR EYES, BUT YOU DON'T—SO WATCH YOUR CREDITS!

You will need black and white frosting.

Spread black frosting over top of cupcake. Place a coupler inside a pastry bag. Using a table knife, make a thin stripe of black frosting inside the pastry bag. Carefully spoon white frosting into the bag without disrupting the black stripe of frosting. Twist bag closed and place a small star tip on the coupler. Use a toothpick to outline the face of Muftak. Fill in the rest of the cupcake top by piping long star peaks that look like fur (they will be two-toned). Place 4 mini round candy-coated chocolate pieces on face for eyes. If desired, place a dot of black frosting in center of eyes. Break a piece of pretzel and insert into creature's mouth.

MYO

TOUGH-GUY MYO IS ALWAYS ITCHING FOR A FIGHT! HE'S AN EXPERT IN SURVIVAL TECHNIQUES, SO YOU DEFINITELY WANT HIM ON YOUR SIDE IN ANY KIND OF A SCUFFLE.

You will need white, black, and green frosting.

Spread green frosting on top of cupcakes. With a small spatula or knife, make indentations for his cheeks. Let dry for a few minutes. Lay a damp paper towel over top of cupcake and press lightly, then remove to create texture. Use a toothpick to outline wrinkles on forehead. Place a small amount of green frosting in a pastry bag. Snip the tip of bag and pipe a nose outline. Place a small amount of white frosting in a pastry bag. Snip the tip of bag and pipe a single eye and some teeth. Use some black frosting to pipe pupil of eye. For beard, just before serving, attach small pieces of cotton candy onto sides of his chin. (If icing is dry, you may need to pipe a bit of green icing onto the chin area to stick.)

FIGRIN D'AN

PUT YOUR HANDS TOGETHER FOR FIGRIN D'AN AND THE MODAL NODES! AS LEADER OF THE HOUSE BAND AT THE MOS EISLEY CANTINA, THIS TALENTED MULTI-INSTRUMENTALIST CAN PLAY UP A SANDSTORM ON THE KLOO HORN AND GASAN STRING DRUM.

You will need pale yellow and pale gray (optional) frosting and peach or orange food coloring.

Spread pale yellow frosting over cupcakes, making frosting as smooth as possible. Fold a damp paper towel and place a dot of peach food coloring on the towel. Run the edge of a table knife through food coloring. Use the edge of knife to score the facial lines on top of cupcake. When the knife gets frosting on it, wipe clean and run through food coloring again. Use tip of knife to make eye sockets on face. Place 2 round black candies in eye sockets. For flute, cut a 2-inch piece of licorice and place on side of face. Cut a small sliver of black licorice and place on face where mouthpiece would be. Optional: Pipe small gray lines of icing or frosting onto flute for detail. (This could be the two-tone icing used for Muftak.)

FROZEN WORLDS

The white and cool-blue worlds of Hoth and Starkiller Base offer delights in tune with their landscapes—airy meringues, ice cream sandwiches, cream puffs, and more.

SNOWDRIFT MERINGUES

These peppermint-flavored meringues are as cool as a new snow. The key to the lightest, crispiest meringues is to bake at a low temperature and to leave them in the oven (turn the oven off!) after baking time for 2 hours to completely dry out.

ACTIVE TIME 25 MIN   TOTAL TIME 3 HRS 25 MIN   MAKES ABOUT 20 MERINGUES

½ cup granulated sugar
½ cup superfine sugar
 4 egg whites
⅛ teaspoon cream of tartar
½ teaspoon peppermint
   extract
   Silver luster dust

1. Heat oven to 250°F. Line two large rimmed baking sheets with parchment paper. In a small bowl stir together the granulated and superfine sugars; set aside.

2. In a large bowl beat egg whites with a hand mixer until foamy. Add cream of tartar. Beat on high speed 2 more minutes or until soft peaks form. While beating on high speed, gradually add sugar mixture, 1 tablespoon at a time, until stiff peaks form. Beat in peppermint extract.

3. Drop meringue mixture by spoonfuls onto prepared baking sheets, forming little clouds 1 inch apart. Sprinkle clouds of meringue lightly with silver luster dust. Bake for 1 hour or just until firm and dry to touch but not brown. Turn oven off, leaving oven door shut. Allow meringues to cool and completely dry in oven for 2 hours.

   TO STORE: Store in an airtight container at room temperature.

HOTH COCOA CREAM PUFFS

This beverage, perfect for the frigid temperatures of Hoth, morphs into an airy pastry with cinnamon-spiced chocolate pudding. No hot chocolate pods or multiprocessors needed!

ACTIVE TIME 1 HR   TOTAL TIME 1 HR 25 MIN   MAKES 48 2-INCH CREAM PUFFS

FILLING

- 4 teaspoons instant coffee granules (optional)
- 1 tablespoon boiling water (optional)
- 1 (3.4-ounce) package instant chocolate pudding
- 1 cup heavy cream
- ½ cup whole milk
- ½ teaspoon ground cinnamon

CREAM PUFFS

- ¾ cup water
- 6 tablespoons unsalted butter, diced
- 1 tablespoon granulated sugar
- ¼ teaspoon salt
- 1 cup all-purpose flour
- 4 large eggs, divided

TOPPING

- 1 (7-ounce) jar marshmallow creme

1. **For the Filling:** Dissolve the coffee in the boiling water, if using; set aside. In large bowl combine the pudding mix, cream, milk, cinnamon, and coffee mixture, if using. With a mixer, beat on low speed for 2 minutes. Cover and refrigerate until ready to use.

2. Preheat oven to 400°F and line two rimmed baking sheets with parchment paper. Brush the parchment lightly with water.

3. **For the Cream Puffs:** Combine the water, butter, sugar, and salt in a saucepan. Bring to a boil over medium heat, stirring occasionally to melt the butter. As soon as it boils, remove the pan from the heat and add the flour all at once. Stir until it forms a ball around the base of the spoon. Return to low heat and dry the paste out slightly, stirring constantly, about 30 seconds. A dry film will form on the bottom of the pan. Cool the paste 10 minutes.

4. Whisk one egg in a bowl and set aside. Stir remaining eggs, one at a time, into dough, beating thoroughly after each addition.

5. Drop dough by tablespoons onto prepared baking sheets, spacing them a couple inches apart. Try to make them as neat as possible and the same size. With your fingertips dipped into the extra beaten egg, gently smooth out the tops of the cream puffs. Discard remaining egg mixture.

6. Bake at 400°F for 15 minutes. Reduce heat to 350°F and bake 10 to 13 minutes more or until golden. The cream puff sides should be dry and not soft. Remove from oven and transfer pastries to a rack; cool completely.

7. **To Assemble:** Use a serrated knife to slice each cream puff in half horizontally. With a spoon, top each puff bottom with a tablespoon of filling; replace top. Repeat with remaining cream puffs.

8. Top each puff with about a teaspoon of marshmallow creme. With a kitchen torch, toast marshmallow evenly to lightly brown. (Or put under the broiler for 30 seconds to 1 minute, watching constantly to avoid burning.)

R2-D2 ICE CREAM CAKE

This special-occasion cake is the bombe! (In baking, a "bombe" is an ice cream-filled sponge cake shaped like a dome.) This cake takes some effort, but any intrepid baker who makes it honors the adventurous, spunky droid it's named after.

ACTIVE TIME 1 HR 30 MIN   TOTAL TIME 4 HRS 30 MIN   MAKES 1 CAKE (12 SLICES)

3 large eggs
Vegetable oil, for greasing the pan
⅓ cup all-purpose flour
½ teaspoon baking powder
½ teaspoon vanilla extract
¼ cup + ⅓ cup granulated sugar, divided
Powdered sugar
1 (1.5-ounce) can blue food color spray
1 (1.5-ounce) can silver food color spray
1 quart vanilla ice cream, softened
1 chocolate sandwich cookie, deconstructed (optional)
1 red gumdrop (optional)
Gray frosting (optional)
Silver dragees (optional)

1. Separate egg whites and yolks. Allow to stand at room temperature for 30 minutes. Meanwhile, grease a 13×9-inch baking sheet. Line bottom of pan with parchment paper. Grease paper. Set aside. In a medium bowl stir together flour and baking powder; set aside.

2. Preheat oven to 375°F. In a medium mixing bowl beat egg yolks and vanilla with a hand mixer on high speed about 5 minutes or until thick and lemon color. Gradually beat in the ¼ cup sugar, beating on high speed until sugar is almost dissolved.

3. Thoroughly wash beaters. In another bowl beat egg whites on medium speed until soft peaks form. Gradually beat in the ⅓ cup sugar, beating until stiff peaks form. Fold the egg yolk mixture into beaten egg whites. Sprinkle flour mixture over egg mixture; fold in gently just until combined. Spread batter evenly in prepared pan.

4. Bake for 12 to 15 minutes or until cake springs back when lightly touched. Immediately loosen edges of cake from pan and turn cake out onto a towel sprinkled with powdered sugar. Remove parchment paper. Cool completely.

continued on page 48

continued from page 47

5. To assemble cake, line a 1½-quart bowl with plastic wrap. Cut half of the cake into six 3-inch triangles. Cut remaining cake into eight rectangles. Spray triangles with blue spray. Spray rectangles with silver spray. Press cake triangles, pointed-side down and color side facing out, into bottom of lined bowl, forming a circle and overlapping cake if necessary. Press rectangles of cake around sides of lined bowl, fitting together tightly. Cut cake pieces if necessary to fit. Freeze cake-lined bowl at least 1 hour.

6. Line cake bowl with plastic wrap. Spread softened ice cream into plastic-covered cake-lined bowl, pressing to fill bowl and eliminate any gaps. Cover and freeze 2 hours or until firm.

7. When firm, lift plastic wrap and remove from ice cream. Return ice cream to cake-lined bowl.

8. Press ice cream gently into cake. Carefully invert cake and ice cream onto a serving plate. Remove plastic wrap from cake. If desired, working quickly, pipe gray frosting around the seam where the blue triangles and silver rectangles meet and around the base of the cake. Using additional frosting, attach the two halves of a chocolate cookie, the gum drop, and silver dragees for details, if desired.

TO STORE: Store cake in freezer until ready to serve.

TIE FIGHTER ICE CREAM SANDWICHES

The scream of an approaching fleet of TIE fighters may have struck fear in the hearts of any enemy of the Empire, but you'll only make friends when you build a batch of these frozen treats.

ACTIVE TIME 2 HRS   TOTAL TIME 6 HRS   MAKES 10 ICE CREAM SANDWICHES

¼ cup unsalted butter, softened

½ cup chocolate-hazelnut spread

1 cup granulated sugar

½ teaspoon baking powder

1 large egg

¼ cup whole milk

1 teaspoon vanilla extract

2¾ cups all-purpose flour, plus more for dusting

½ cup semisweet chocolate chips

1 teaspoon shortening

1 quart desired ice cream (chocolate, mint chip, or chocolate chip)

1. In a large mixing bowl, beat butter and chocolate-hazelnut spread with a hand mixer on medium to high speed for 30 seconds or until softened. Add sugar and baking powder. Beat until combined, scraping sides of bowl occasionally. Beat in egg, milk, and vanilla until combined. Beat in as much flour as you can with the mixer. Stir in remaining flour with a wooden spoon.

2. Shape dough into a disk. Wrap dough in plastic wrap and chill for 4 to 24 hours.

3. Preheat oven to 375°F. Line two rimmed baking sheets with parchment paper. On a lightly floured surface, roll out chilled dough to 20×12-inch rectangle (¼-inch thickness). Using a knife (or pizza cutter) and the wing template (page 53), cut dough into 20 wings. Transfer wings with a spatula to prepared baking sheets. Prick each cookie several times with a fork. Bake for 8 to 10 minutes or until cookies are firm in center. Let cool on the pan for 5 minutes. Transfer to a wire rack to cool completely.

continued on page 52

continued from page 50

4. Place chocolate chips and shortening in a small microwave-safe bowl. Microwave on high for 45 seconds, then stir. Microwave for 30 seconds more or until chocolate is melted, stirring every 30 seconds.

5. Place melted chocolate in a decorating bag. Snip tip of bag to make a tiny opening. Decorate tops of cookies with piped chocolate to resemble a TIE fighter wing. Chill cookies until ready to fill with ice cream, at least 30 minutes.

6. Place a small, round scoop (¼ cup) of ice cream between two chilled cookies and very gently press together to avoid breaking the cookies. (The ice cream should stay just in middle of the sandwich.) Store in freezer.

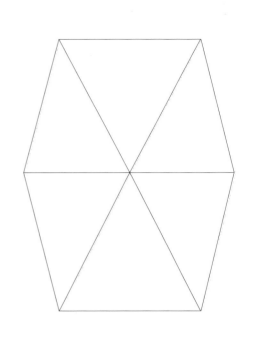

MIND TRICK COOKIES

Just as Rey performed a Jedi mind trick to free herself on Starkiller Base,
you can fool your friends and family with these snowy-white cookies.
Convince them that they're coconut, even though they're also chocolate.

ACTIVE TIME 1 HR   TOTAL TIME 1 HR 30 MIN   MAKES 72 COOKIES

¾ cup unsalted butter, at room temperature

½ cup powdered sugar

1 cup all-purpose flour

¼ cup cornstarch

¼ teaspoon salt

1 cup sweetened shredded coconut, finely pulverized in a small food processor

6 teaspoons clear chocolate extract, divided

1 (16-ounce) can white frosting

Coarse white sanding sugar (see note below)

1. Heat oven to 325°F. In a large bowl, beat butter and powdered sugar with a hand mixer until pale and fluffy. With mixer on low speed, beat in flour, cornstarch, salt, coconut, and 3 teaspoons of the extract until smooth. Wrap dough in plastic wrap and chill 15 to 20 minutes or until dough is firm enough to handle.

2. Shape dough into 1-inch balls and place on an ungreased baking sheet about 2 inches apart.

3. Bake 12 to 15 minutes or until cookies are firm to the touch and just lightly browned around edges. Let cool on pan for 5 minutes. Transfer to a cooling rack placed over a sheet pan and let cool completely.

4. Transfer frosting from container to a microwavable bowl. Heat frosting in the microwave on high for 30 seconds. Stir the frosting to check consistency. If necessary, heat for another 10 seconds to create a glaze that is loose enough to spoon over cookies without completely running off. Stir in remaining 3 teaspoons clear chocolate extract.

5. Using a spoon, coat the cookies on the cooling rack with the frosting glaze covered completely. Sprinkle with sanding sugar and let stand to set frosting.

NOTE: Instead of the white sanding sugar, you can use white jimmies, small white nonpareils, or winter-theme sprinkles to decorate the cookies.

WON-TAUN TUNDRA TREATS

No tauntaun—or any other tundra-dwelling creature, human
or otherwise—will be able to resist these crispy pastry purses
filled with chocolate-hazelnut spread and banana slices.

ACTIVE TIME 30 MIN   TOTAL TIME 50 MIN   MAKES 16 WONTONS

2 tablespoons
granulated sugar

2 teaspoons ground
cinnamon

16 wonton wrappers

5 tablespoons chocolate-
hazelnut spread

1 large ripe banana, sliced
very thin

1 large egg beaten with
1 tablespoon water

¼ cup powdered sugar

1. Preheat oven to 375°F. Line a large rimmed baking sheet with
parchment paper. In a small bowl, stir together the sugar and
cinnamon; set aside.

2. Separate four wonton wrappers and place on a clean work
surface. Place a scant teaspoon chocolate-hazelnut spread in
the center of each wrapper and top with two slices of banana.
Sprinkle with a good pinch of the sugar-cinnamon mixture.

3. Working with one wonton at a time, dip your finger into the
egg mixture and run it along all four sides of the wrapper.
Bring two diagonal corners up to meet together, then bring
the remaining corners up to meet at the center. Pinch the
seams to seal. Repeat this process for the remaining wontons.

4. Place the prepared wontons on the baking sheet. Brush the
outside of each wonton with the egg wash. Bake for 13 to
15 minutes or until crisp and golden brown.

5. Let cool for 5 minutes on the baking sheet. With a fine sifter,
dust the wontons with powdered sugar.

SUGAR COOKIE CUTOUTS
WITH PRINCESS LEIA'S ROYAL ICING

Transform cookie dough into a cast of galactic characters with some cool tools and an easy-to-work-with icing that turns out smooth and flawless every time.

ROLLED SUGAR COOKIES

MAKES 30 COOKIES

2 ¼ cups all-purpose flour, plus more for dusting
½ teaspoon baking powder
¼ teaspoon salt
¾ cup butter, softened
¾ cup granulated sugar
1 large egg, room temperature
2 teaspoons pure vanilla extract

1. In a medium bowl, whisk together flour, baking powder, and salt.

2. In a large bowl, beat butter and sugar with an electric mixer on high speed until smooth and creamy, about 2 minutes. Add the egg and vanilla, and beat on high speed until combined, about 1 minute, scraping down sides of bowl as necessary.

3. Add the flour mixture to the butter mixture and mix on low until combined. (Dough will be soft; if it seems too soft and sticky for rolling, add an additional 1 tablespoon flour.)

4. Divide dough into two equal pieces. Place each portion on a lightly floured sheet of parchment paper. With a lightly floured rolling pin, roll the dough out to ¼-inch thickness.

5. Lightly dust one of the pieces of dough with flour. Place a sheet of parchment on top. Place the second piece of rolled-out dough on top. Cover with plastic wrap and chill in the refrigerator for 1 to 2 hours.

6. Preheat oven to 350°F. Line two large rimmed baking sheets with parchment paper. Carefully place one piece of dough on a lightly floured surface. Cut cookies and place 3 inches apart on one of the prepared pans, then remove extra dough. Reroll and continue cutting until all dough is used. Repeat with second piece of dough.

7. Bake 11 to 12 minutes or until lightly browned on the edges. Cool cookies on baking sheets for 5 minutes, then transfer to a rack to cool completely before decorating.

ROYAL ICING

MAKES 2 ½ CUPS

1 ¾ cups powdered sugar
4 ½ teaspoons meringue powder
¼ teaspoon cream of tartar
¼ cup warm water
½ teaspoon pure vanilla extract
Paste or gel food coloring (brown, green, juniper, peach, black, blue, red)

1. In a large bowl, whisk together powdered sugar, meringue powder, and cream of tartar. Add warm water and vanilla. Beat on low speed with an electric mixer until combined. Beat on high speed for 7 to 10 minutes or until mixture is very stiff. Divide into seven portions and tint with food coloring (you will only need a tiny amount of blue and red). Keep covered.

2. **To Decorate:** Transfer about two-thirds of an icing color to a small bowl. Stir in a small amount of water until thin enough to drizzle. Place in a pastry bag and snip a very small opening at tip. Pipe an outline of icing onto cookie, then fill with more icing. Use a toothpick to spread. Repeat with remaining color. Tint thicker icing gray and darker black, peach, green, blue, and red. Fill pastry bags fitted with very small round tips and pipe details on each cookie. Allow to dry.

Note: *Star Wars* cookie cutters are available at williams-sonoma.com.

GREEN WORLDS

The lush forests, jungles, and mountains of Endor, Ahch-To, Ajan Kloss, and beyond create the inspiration for these marshmallow-filled moon pies, energy bars to fuel the Resistance, and special-occasion cakes.

WICKET MOON PIES

These treats are perfect for taking to the forest moon of Endor, which is inhabited by the small-but-mighty Ewoks. The same might be said for these fiercely good chocolate-dipped cinnamon-graham sandwich cookies stuffed with marshmallow creme.

ACTIVE TIME 1 HR   TOTAL TIME 3 HRS 15 MIN   MAKES 16 SANDWICH COOKIES

1 cup all-purpose flour

⅓ cup whole wheat flour

½ teaspoon ground cinnamon

½ cup unsalted butter, room temperature

⅔ cup granulated sugar

1 large egg yolk

2 tablespoons whole milk

1 teaspoon vanilla extract

1 cup marshmallow creme, plus additional for eyes

1 (11-ounce) bag + ½ cup milk-chocolate chips (for ears)

2 teaspoons shortening

Chocolate sprinkles (jimmies)

½ cup dark chocolate chips or semisweet chocolate chips

Mini milk chocolate chips

1. In a medium bowl, stir together all-purpose flour, whole wheat flour, and cinnamon; set aside. In a mixing bowl, beat butter with a hand mixer for 30 seconds. Add sugar and beat well. Beat in egg yolk, milk, and vanilla. Add flour mixture to butter mixture. Beat until well combined. Wrap dough in plastic wrap and chill 2 hours or until easy to handle.

2. Preheat oven to 350°F. Line two large rimmed baking sheets with parchment paper. Shape dough into thirty-two 1-inch balls. Place balls 1 inch apart on baking sheets. Flatten balls to ½-inch thickness. Bake about 10 minutes or until firm. Let cool on pan for 5 minutes. Transfer to wire racks to cool.

3. Place a small spoonful of marshmallow creme on the bottom sides of half of the cookies. Place another cookie on top to make cookie sandwiches; set aside.

4. Place the 11 ounces of milk chocolate chips and the shortening in a small heat-proof bowl. Place bowl over a small saucepan with an inch of water. (Bowl should not touch water in pan.) Heat pan over medium heat while occasionally stirring chocolate until melted. Reduce heat to low.

5. Dip sandwich cookies in melted chocolate, allowing excess to drip off. Place on parchment paper. While chocolate is still wet, sprinkle each cookie with some chocolate jimmies and place two dark chocolate chips (upside-down) for eyes. Place a mini chocolate chip for a nose and two milk-chocolate chips for ears. Place some marshmallow creme in a pastry bag. Snip a small hole at the end. Pipe white dots on the eyes. (Make one cookie at a time, placing in the refrigerator to firm up as soon as they're finished.)

FOREST OF ENDOR LOG CAKE

Although this is definitely not a lightspeed recipe, you'll be richly rewarded for taking the time and effort to make this incredible jelly roll–style cake filled with matcha cream and decorated with meringue mushrooms and candy ferns.

ACTIVE TIME 2 HRS · TOTAL TIME 2 HRS 15 MIN · MAKES 1 LOG CAKE (12 SLICES)

CAKE

- 4 large eggs
- Vegetable oil, for greasing pan
- ⅓ cup all-purpose flour
- 2 tablespoons unsweetened dark cocoa powder, plus additional for dusting
- 1 teaspoon baking powder
- ½ teaspoon vanilla extract
- ⅓ + ½ cup granulated sugar, divided
- Powdered sugar

MERINGUE MUSHROOMS

- 2 egg whites
- ⅛ teaspoon cream of tartar
- ½ cup granulated sugar
- 2 ounces chocolate candy coating or chocolate chips
- Unsweetened dark cocoa powder (optional)

FERN FRONDS

- 2 ounces green candy melts

MATCHA CREAM FILLING

- 4 ounces cream cheese, softened
- 3 tablespoons granulated sugar
- 2 tablespoons fine matcha powder
- 1 (8-ounce) container thawed whipped topping

1. **For the cake:** Separate egg yolks from whites and allow to stand at room temperature for 30 minutes. Meanwhile, grease a 15×10-inch baking sheet. Line bottom of pan with waxed paper or parchment paper. Grease paper. Set aside. In a medium bowl stir together flour, the 2 tablespoons cocoa powder, and the baking powder; set aside.

2. Preheat oven to 375°F. In a medium mixing bowl beat egg yolks and vanilla with a hand mixer on high speed about 5 minutes or until thick and lemon color. Gradually beat in the ⅓ cup granulated sugar, beating on high speed until sugar is almost dissolved.

3. Thoroughly wash beaters. In another bowl beat egg whites on medium speed until soft peaks form. Gradually beat in the ½ cup granulated sugar, beating until stiff peaks form. Fold egg yolk mixture into beaten egg whites. Sprinkle the flour mixture over egg mixture; fold in gently just until combined. Spread batter evenly in prepared pan.

4. Bake for 12 to 15 minutes or until cake springs back when lightly touched. Meanwhile, dust a clean kitchen towel randomly with powdered sugar and remaining cocoa powder. When cake is done, immediately loosen edges of cake from pan and turn cake out onto dusted towel. Remove waxed paper. Roll towel and warm cake into a spiral, starting from a short side of the cake. Cool on a wire rack. Turn oven down to 250°F. Meanwhile, prepare meringue mushrooms, fern fronds, and matcha cream filling.

continued on page 67

continued from page 64

5. **For the Meringue Mushrooms:** Line a baking sheet with parchment paper. In a mixing bowl beat egg whites with cream of tartar with a hand mixer until soft peaks form. Very gradually beat in the granulated sugar until stiff peaks form. Place a large round tip in a pastry bag and fill the bag with meringue. Pipe the meringue into 12 short mushroom-cap shapes on the prepared pan. (Use a damp finger to tap down any peaks.) For the stems, pipe meringue into cylinder shapes by pulling the tip straight up. Bake in the 250°F oven for 30 to 40 minutes or until pieces are dry to the touch. Let cool before peeling from parchment paper. Place chocolate candy coating in a microwave-safe bowl. Microwave on high for 30 seconds; stir. Repeat until chocolate is melted. Poke a small hole in the bottom of a mushroom cap. Spread melted chocolate over the bottom of the cap. Dip the tip of a stem in the chocolate and press lightly into the hole. Repeat with other caps and stems. If desired, dust lightly with cocoa powder. Set aside until set.

6. **For the Fern Fronds:** Melt the green candy melts. Place in a disposable decorating bag. Snip a tiny opening in the end of the pastry bag. Pipe small, 1- to 3-inch fern shapes on waxed paper or on parchment. Chill until very firm. When ready to decorate, carefully peel candy fronds from paper.

7. **For the Matcha Cream Filling:** In a mixing bowl beat the cream cheese with a hand mixer for 30 seconds. Beat in the granulated sugar and matcha powder. Fold in the whipped topping.

8. **To Assemble the Log:** Unroll cake; remove towel. Spread cake with Matcha Cream Filling to within 1 inch of edges. Roll up cake. Cover and chill at least 2 hours. To decorate cake, trim a 1 ½-inch slice off each end. Press the slices onto opposite sides of the cake roll to make branches.

9. Arrange mushrooms and fern fronds around cake as desired.

MON MOTHMA'S MINI FOCACCIA

Rebel leader Mon Mothma's home planet of Chandrila is known for its sweet peppers, which make for a great topping when baked onto warm bread. These focaccia are best eaten while saving the galaxy from the tyranny of the Empire!

ACTIVE TIME 30 MIN   TOTAL TIME 1 HR   MAKES 6 MINI FOCACCIA

2¼ cups all-purpose flour

1 tablespoon active dry yeast

1 teaspoon salt

1 teaspoon granulated sugar

1 teaspoon garlic powder

1 teaspoon dried Italian seasoning

1 cup warm water (120°F)

3 tablespoons olive oil, divided, plus more for greasing

1 cup grape tomatoes, halved

6 mini sweet peppers, thinly sliced into rings

3 green onions, sliced

Chopped fresh herbs (parsley, rosemary, basil, and/or thyme)

6 pitted black or green olives, halved or sliced

3 tablespoons grated Parmesan cheese

1. In a large bowl combine flour, yeast, salt, sugar, garlic powder, and Italian seasoning. Stir in warm water and 1 tablespoon of the oil. Stir with a wooden spoon until well combined. Turn out onto a floured surface. Knead with hands until smooth and elastic, about 4 minutes. Place in a lightly oiled bowl and turn over to coat with oil. Cover with a damp cloth and let rise in a warm place for 20 minutes.

2. Preheat oven to 450°F. Punch down dough and divide into six portions. Shape portions into balls. On a floured surface, press dough balls into ½-inch-thick rounds or ovals that are 6 inches in diameter. Place dough circles on two greased baking sheets. Brush tops with remaining 2 tablespoons oil. Top with tomatoes, pepper slices, green onions, fresh herbs, and olives. Sprinkle with grated cheese.

3. Bake for 10 to 15 minutes or until golden brown.

RESISTANCE RATION BARS

When you're trying to save the galaxy from the First Order, you might miss a meal or two. These portable, protein-packed bars will fuel you through even the most harrowing skirmish.

ACTIVE TIME 30 MIN   TOTAL TIME 1 HR   MAKES 24 BARS

Nonstick cooking spray

3 cups rolled oats

1 cup mixed nuts (slivered almonds, cashew halves, chopped macadamias, pistachios)

½ cup salted sunflower seeds or pepitas

6 tablespoons butter

⅔ cup dark brown sugar

½ cup honey

2 teaspoons vanilla extract

1 teaspoon salt

1 cup chopped assorted dried fruit (raisins, apricots, pineapple, dates)

½ cup unsweetened coconut flakes

1. Preheat oven to 350°F. Line a 13×9-inch baking sheet with foil, leaving a 2-inch overhang on two sides. Coat the foil with cooking spray; set aside. Combine oats, nuts, and seeds on a rimmed baking sheet. Bake for 10 minutes; remove and set aside.

2. Meanwhile, in a large saucepan melt butter over medium heat. Add brown sugar and honey; stir to dissolve. Remove pan from heat and stir in vanilla and salt. Stir in the toasted oat mixture, dried fruit, and coconut; stir to thoroughly coat.

3. Spread evenly in pan and press in using damp fingers. Bake about 20 minutes or until lightly browned. Transfer baking sheet to a rack and let cool completely in pan.

4. When cool, gently lift the bars by the foil overhang to a cutting board. Remove foil and cut into 24 bars.

MEILOORUN HAND PIES

Beloved by General Hera Syndulla of the Rebel Alliance, the prickly orange meiloorun fruit is delicious but rare. If you can't get your hands on any, you can use fresh or frozen peaches in these hand pies.

ACTIVE TIME 1 HR   TOTAL TIME 1 HR 20 MIN   MAKES 12 HAND PIES

2½ cups all-purpose flour, plus more for dusting

½ teaspoon salt

1 cup cold unsalted butter, cut up

⅓ cup sour cream

1 tablespoon lemon juice

⅔ cup ice water

⅓ cup granulated sugar

2 teaspoons cornstarch

¼ teaspoon ground cinnamon

⅛ teaspoon ground ginger

3 fresh peaches, peeled, pitted, and chopped (or 2 cups frozen peaches, chopped)

1 egg yolk

2 tablespoons water

Coarse sugar

1. In a mixing bowl, stir together flour and salt. Using a pastry blender, cut in butter until mixture is the size of coarse crumbs. In a small bowl, combine sour cream, lemon juice, and ice water. Gradually add to flour mixture, tossing together with a fork until evenly moistened. Gather dough into a ball and wrap with plastic wrap. Chill while making filling.

2. For filling, in a small saucepan combine granulated sugar, cornstarch, cinnamon, and ginger. Stir in chopped peaches. Cook and stir over medium heat just until mixture is bubbly. Remove from heat and cool.

3. To assemble, line a large rimmed baking sheet with parchment paper. Divide dough into 12 balls. On a floured surface, roll out dough to ⅛-inch thickness. Spoon about 2 tablespoons of peach filling onto center of each dough circle.

4. In a small bowl beat together egg yolk and the 2 tablespoons water. Very lightly brush edges of dough with egg mixture. Fold circles in half and place on prepared baking sheet. Use tines of a fork to press and seal edges of pies. Brush pies with more egg mixture and sprinkle with coarse sugar. Chill while preheating oven to 375°F.

5. Bake for 20 minutes or until golden brown.

GREEN MILK CAKE WITH CHOCOLATE DRIZZLE

Inspired by the green milk of thala-sirens, you'll want to take a slice of this chocolate-drizzled, pistachio-flavored cake with you before traveling to Ahch-To.

ACTIVE TIME 30 MIN   TOTAL TIME 1 HR 30 MIN   MAKES 1 CAKE (12 TO 16 SLICES)

STREUSEL
- ½ cup packed brown sugar
- ½ cup roasted and salted pistachio nuts, chopped
- 2 teaspoons ground cinnamon

CAKE
- 1 (15.25-ounce) package white cake mix
- 1 (3.4-ounce) package instant pistachio pudding mix
- 4 large eggs
- 1 cup sour cream
- ½ cup vegetable oil
- ½ teaspoon vanilla extract
- 8 drops liquid green food coloring

TOPPING
- 1 (16-ounce) container prepared chocolate frosting
- Chopped roasted and salted pistachio nuts

1. Preheat oven to 350°F. Grease and flour a 10-cup Bundt pan.

2. **For the Streusel**: Combine brown sugar, pistachio nuts, and cinnamon in a small bowl; set aside.

3. **For the Cake:** Combine the cake mix and pudding mix in a large mixing bowl. Make an indentation in the center and add eggs, sour cream, oil, vanilla, and food coloring. Blend ingredients with a hand mixer on medium speed for 2 minutes, stopping and scraping bowl as needed. (The batter will be thick.)

4. Spoon half of the batter into the prepared pan. Sprinkle the streusel over the batter, being careful to keep the streusel from the edges (it might stick to the pan). Carefully cover the streusel with the remaining cake batter.

5. Bake 1 hour or until cake springs back when lightly touched. Cool for 15 minutes in pan before inverting onto a wire rack to cool completely.

6. **For the Topping:** When the cake is cool, heat frosting in a microwave-safe bowl on high for 30 seconds. Stir the frosting to check consistency. If necessary, heat for another 10 seconds to create a pourable frosting. Pour soft frosting over the cake to drape down the sides. Sprinkle with pistachio nuts.

7. Cool until drizzle sets up before serving.

REY'S TRAINING COURSE ENERGY BITES

After leaping over chasms and dodging the blasts of a training remote—not to mention resisting Kylo Ren's attempts to interfere—it took Rey every ounce of strength she had to run the Ajan Kloss training course. These energy bites provide the boost you'd need to make it through in one piece.

ACTIVE TIME 30 MIN   TOTAL TIME 1 HR 30 MIN   MAKES 30 BALLS

2 cups quick-cooking oats

2 cups unsweetened coconut flakes

1 cup sliced almonds

¼ cup wheat germ, toasted

3 tablespoons mini chocolate chips

1 teaspoon ground cinnamon

½ teaspoon salt

1 cup creamy almond butter, stirred

¾ cup pure maple syrup

1 teaspoon vanilla extract

1. Line a large rimmed baking sheet with waxed paper or parchment paper. In a mixing bowl combine oats, coconut, almonds, wheat germ, chocolate chips, cinnamon, and salt. Stir until blended.

2. In a small bowl whisk together almond butter, syrup, and vanilla.

3. Pour the liquid ingredients into the dry ingredients. Mix together until evenly combined and no dry oats remain.

4. Divide into 30 equal portions and roll each into a ball. Place on the prepared pan. Cover with plastic wrap and chill for at least 1 hour or overnight.

TAKE THEM WITH YOU: Individual balls may be wrapped in plastic wrap. Energy balls keep well for a couple of days at room temperature. Or store individually wrapped balls in a freezer-safe bag in the freezer for several months.

PUFFER PIG POCKET PIZZAS

Puffer pigs grow to more than three times their size when frightened.
These puff pastry pockets stuffed with pork sausage and two
kinds of cheese do the same thing when baked to crispy, melty
deliciousness. Serve with warm pizza sauce for dipping.

ACTIVE TIME 30 MIN   TOTAL TIME 50 MIN   MAKES 8 POCKET PIZZAS

2 large eggs

1 tablespoon water

1 pound Italian pork
sausage, cooked,
crumbled, and drained

1 cup ricotta cheese

1 cup shredded mozzarella
cheese

1 teaspoon Italian
seasoning

½ teaspoon salt

All-purpose flour

1 (17.3-ounce) package
frozen puff pastry, thawed
according to package
directions

1 (15-ounce) jar prepared
pizza sauce, warmed

1. Preheat oven to 400°F. Line two large rimmed baking sheets
   with parchment paper. In a small bowl whisk one of the eggs
   and water together to make an egg wash; set aside.

2. For the filling, in a medium bowl combine sausage, ricotta,
   mozzarella, remaining egg, Italian seasoning, and salt;
   set aside.

3. Sprinkle a work surface with some flour. Unfold one thawed
   pastry sheet on the work surface. Roll the pastry sheet into
   a 12-inch square. Cut into four pieces. Brush edges of each
   square with prepared egg wash. Place ¼ cup filling in the
   center of each square. Fold the pastry over the filling to form
   triangles. Press edges and crimp with a fork to firmly seal.
   With fork tines, prick each pastry to allow steam to escape.
   Repeat with the remaining pastry sheet.

4. Place the filled pastries on prepared baking sheets. Brush
   the outside of pastries with the remaining egg wash mixture.
   Bake for 20 minutes or until golden brown.

5. Let cool for 10 minutes before serving. Serve with pizza sauce
   as a dipper.

LIFE DAY CAKE

Fuel up for the journey to the Tree of Life with this fruit- and nut-studded fruitcake-style bread—perfect for any Wookiee's Life Day celebration.

ACTIVE TIME 30 MIN TOTAL TIME 2 HRS MAKES 1 LOAF (12 TO 16 SLICES)

Vegetable oil, for greasing pan

8 ounces sour cream

1 teaspoon baking soda

1 cup chopped dried pineapple

2 cups golden raisins

½ cup candied red cherries

1 cup chopped walnuts

2 cups all-purpose flour, divided

½ cup unsalted butter, softened

1 cup granulated sugar

3 large eggs

1 tablespoon orange zest

½ teaspoon salt

2 to 4 tablespoons rum or orange juice

Powdered Sugar Icing (optional)

1. Preheat oven to 325°F. Grease a 9×5-inch loaf pan. Line bottom and sides with parchment paper. In a small bowl combine sour cream and baking soda. In a large bowl combine dried pineapple, raisins, candied cherries, and walnuts. Add ¼ cup of the flour and toss to coat. In another mixing bowl beat butter and sugar with a hand mixer until fluffy. Add eggs, one at a time, and beat well. Beat in orange zest, salt, and sour cream mixture. Add the remaining 1 ¾ cups flour; beat until combined. Stir in fruit-and-nut mixture.

2. Spread batter in prepared pan. Fill another pan with 2 inches of water and place in bottom of oven. Place batter-filled loaf pan in center of oven. Bake for 1½ to 2 hours or until a toothpick inserted in center of cake comes out clean. Cool for 30 minutes in pan on a wire rack. Remove loaf from pan. Cool completely.

3. With a skewer, poke holes in top of cake. Drizzle rum or orange juice slowly over cake to soak in. Wrap in plastic wrap and store at least 1 day or up to 1 week before serving.

4. If desired, drizzle with powdered sugar icing before slicing to serve.

   POWDERED SUGAR ICING: In a medium bowl stir together 1½ cups powdered sugar, 1 tablespoon orange juice, and 1 teaspoon vanilla extract. Add more juice if necessary to reach drizzling consistency.

LOTH-CAT KIBBLE

Inspired by the loth-cats found on the grassy plains of Lothal, this crunchy kibble was created specifically for humans. Crunchy, sweet, and salty, this tasty snack will satisfy most cravings.

ACTIVE TIME 10 MIN   TOTAL TIME 30 MIN   MAKES ABOUT 8 CUPS

1 cup peanut butter chips, divided

½ cup milk chocolate chips

4 tablespoons butter

1 teaspoon salt

½ cup smooth natural peanut butter

4 cups peanut butter–flavor crunchy corn and oat cereal

4 cups regular crunchy corn and oat cereal

2 cups powdered sugar

1. Mix ½ cup peanut butter chips, the milk chocolate chips, butter, and salt together in a microwave-safe bowl. Heat mixture in microwave on 50 percent power, stirring once or twice, until chips are melted and butter is fully incorporated, about 3 minutes. Remove from microwave and stir in peanut butter.

2. Place both cereals in a very large bowl and pour chocolate mixture over. Gently stir to coat all the cereal. Once coated, add powdered sugar and gently stir again to fully coat all the cereal. Spread out onto a large rimmed baking sheet to cool completely.

3. Once cooled, add remaining peanut butter chips and stir to combine.

   TO STORE: Store at room temperature in an airtight container.

FALUMPASET CHEESE-STUFFED SANDWICH

The falumpaset is a valiant beast, famous for towing Gungan battle wagons during the Battle of Naboo. Their milk is also used to produce a delicious form of cheese, which you can stuff inside a loaf of bread, resulting in a sandwich that's perfect for taking on the go. Whether you're packing for a picnic by the lakes of Naboo, or going on the run from the Trade Federation, this sandwich will always make for a wholesome meal.

ACTIVE TIME 30 MIN   TOTAL TIME 1 HR   MAKES 1 SANDWICH (8 TO 10 SERVINGS)

Nonstick cooking spray
All-purpose flour
1 (16-ounce) loaf frozen white bread dough, thawed according to package directions
½ cup butter, room temperature
⅓ cup prepared mustard
¼ cup dried minced onion
2 tablespoons poppy seeds
8 ounces sliced deli ham
8 ounces grated Swiss cheese
1 large egg beaten with 1 tablespoon water
2 tablespoons finely grated Parmesan cheese

1. Heat oven to 350°F. Line a large rimmed baking sheet with parchment paper and coat with nonstick spray; set aside.

2. Lightly sprinkle a work surface with some flour. Roll dough into a 12×16-inch rectangle. Let rest for 10 to 15 minutes.

3. Meanwhile, combine butter, mustard, dried onion, and poppy seeds with a spoon until thoroughly mixed. Spread the butter filling in a 4-inch strip down center of dough (the long way), leaving a 2-inch border top and bottom. Layer ham slices over the filling and top with cheese.

4. On each long side, cut 1 ½-inch-wide strips to within ½ inch of filling. Begin braid by folding top and bottom flaps toward filling. Starting at one end, fold alternating strips at an angle across filling. Continue braiding strips left over right. Finish by pulling last strip over and tucking under braid.

5. Lift braid carefully with both hands and place onto the prepared baking sheet. Brush braid completely with egg mixture and sprinkle with Parmesan cheese.

6. Bake for 30 to 45 minutes or until golden brown. Cover loaf with foil during last 10 minutes, if necessary, to prevent overbrowning.

7. Cool 10 minutes, then slice and serve warm.

KESHIAN SPICE BREAD

In case you couldn't find any Keshian spice on Takodana or Batuu, cinnamon should be a suitable substitute for this sweet treat. Cinnamon swirl and pecan streusel topping makes this quick bread perfect with a cup of warm milk.

ACTIVE TIME 30 MIN   TOTAL TIME 1 HR 20 MIN   MAKES 1 LOAF (10 SLICES)

Vegetable oil, for greasing pan

½ cup unsalted butter, room temperature

1 cup granulated sugar

3 large eggs, room temperature

2 teaspoons vanilla extract

1½ cups all-purpose flour

½ teaspoon salt

½ teaspoon baking soda

½ teaspoon baking powder

⅓ cup sour cream, room temperature

CINNAMON SWIRL

3 tablespoons brown sugar

1 tablespoon ground cinnamon

1 tablespoon buttermilk

TOPPING

¼ cup chopped pecans

2 tablespoons brown sugar

2 teaspoons ground cinnamon

ICING

¼ cup powdered sugar

2 teaspoons buttermilk

1. Preheat oven to 325°F. Grease an 8×4-inch loaf pan and line with parchment paper; set aside.

2. In the bowl of a stand mixer fitted with the paddle attachment, beat together butter and granulated sugar until light and fluffy, about 3 minutes. Beat in eggs, one a time, beating well after each addition and scraping down the sides of the bowl as needed. Beat in vanilla.

3. In a medium bowl whisk together flour, salt, baking soda, and baking powder. With the mixer on low speed, add half of the dry mixture to the butter mixture. Add sour cream and mix. Finally, add the rest of the flour mixture, mixing just until combined.

4. Transfer 1 cup of the batter to a small bowl. Stir in the cinnamon swirl ingredients to combine.

5. Spread 1 cup of the plain batter into the bottom of prepared loaf pan. Drop the cinnamon batter by spoonfuls into the pan. Top with the remaining plain batter and smooth the top. Using a knife, drag through the batter in the pan a few times (lengthwise and from side to side) to create swirls.

6. Combine the topping Ingredients and sprinkle over the loaf.

7. Bake for 50 to 65 minutes or until a skewer inserted in the center of the loaf comes out clean. If loaf starts to become too dark, cover with a piece of foil. Cool loaf in the pan for about 10 minutes, then run a knife around the loaf to loosen it. Remove and place on a rack to cool completely.

8. **For the Icing:** Whisk together the powdered sugar and buttermilk. Drizzle over the loaf.

CITIES & SPACE STATIONS

When you're not flying through the galaxy or navigating the wilds of the snow-packed, green, or desert worlds, hang out in the city (or the ecumenopolis) and share some good food with friends.

CLOUD CITY MARSHMALLOWS

These marshmallows are so light and airy, you'll feel
like you're floating above Cloud City with every bite.

ACTIVE TIME 1 HR   TOTAL TIME 5 HRS   MAKES 48 MARSHMALLOWS

MARSHMALLOWS

Nonstick cooking spray

½ cup ice water

3 (0.25-ounce) envelopes
unflavored gelatin

2 cups granulated sugar

⅔ cup light corn syrup

¼ cup water

¼ teaspoon salt

2 teaspoons clear vanilla
flavoring

8 to 10 drops liquid blue
food coloring

MARSHMALLOW DUST

½ cup powdered sugar

2 tablespoons cornstarch

1. For the marshmallows, line a 13×9-inch baking sheet
with plastic wrap, keeping it as smooth as possible and
overhanging the edges. Coat the plastic wrap with nonstick
spray. Coat a rubber spatula and sharp knife on both sides
with nonstick spray; set aside.

2. Pour the ½ cup ice water into a small mixing bowl. Sprinkle
powdered gelatin over the water. Gently whisk with a fork
until there are no longer any large clumps of gelatin. Allow the
gelatin to sit for 5 minutes.

3. Meanwhile, in a 2-quart heavy saucepan combine sugar, corn
syrup, the ¼ cup water, and salt. Stir constantly over medium
heat until the sugar is dissolved. Increase heat to medium-
high and heat syrup to boiling. Boil, without stirring, until
syrup reaches 240°F on a candy thermometer, about 10 to
15 minutes; remove from heat.

4. Pour the gelatin mixture into the metal bowl of a stand mixer
fitted with a whisk attachment. Slowly and carefully pour
the hot syrup mixture into the bowl. The mixture will foam
and bubble in the bowl. Start by mixing on a low speed and
gradually increase speed to high. Beat until the mixture is
opaque and thick, about 10 to 15 minutes. Add vanilla and
continue to beat mixture on high until thoroughly combined.

5. Pour the marshmallow mixture into the prepared pan.
Quickly smooth top with coated rubber spatula. Drop blue
food coloring randomly on top of the marshmallow mixture.
Using the coated knife, pull the food coloring through the
mixture to create a swirl pattern. Smooth the top. Allow the
marshmallow mixture to cool completely, then cover with
plastic wrap. Set aside for 4 hours or overnight to firm up at
room temperature.

continued on page 92

continued from page 91

6. For the marshmallow dust, mix powdered sugar and cornstarch in a bowl until thoroughly combined. Place a piece of parchment or waxed paper on a work surface; with a fine sifter, cover it with a small amount of the Marshmallow Dust. Remove the plastic wrap from the pan and invert the marshmallow block onto the coated surface. Remove the plastic wrap used to line the pan.

7. With an oiled sharp knife, cut the marshmallows into squares (six rows by eight rows). Respray knife as needed. Gently toss marshmallows, a few at a time, in a bowl with the remaining marshmallow dust and coat all sides.

8. Tap off excess from each marshmallow and store in an airtight container up to 3 weeks at room temperature.

CREATE A CLOUD CITY SERVING PLATTER: You'll need one 10-inch pie plate (2 inches deep), two 11-inch dinner plates, and a cake stand. Turn the cake stand upside-down, and using a hot-glue gun, glue a dinner plate to the base of the cake stand. Now turn the pie plate upside-down and glue to the top of the plate. Turn the last dinner plate over and glue it to the bottom of the pie plate. Cover the base of the cake stand with batting.

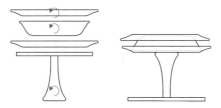

CORUSCANT CROISSANTS

Only in a planet-wide city as cultured as Coruscant—hub of the galaxy—
will you find something as fancy as these miniature croissants filled with a
cocoa-cinnamon spiral. Make the dough up to one day ahead.

ACTIVE TIME 1 HR   TOTAL TIME 6 HRS 15 MIN   MAKES 32 MINI CROISSANTS

DOUGH

- 1 cup warm whole milk (110 °F)
- 1 tablespoon granulated sugar
- 1 package (2¼ teaspoons) active dry yeast
- 1 cup all-purpose flour, plus more for dusting
- ¾ cup whole milk
- 1½ teaspoons salt
- ¼ cup granulated sugar
- 1 large egg, beaten
- ½ cup unsalted butter, melted
- 4 cups all-purpose flour
- 1 cup cold unsalted butter, cut up

FILLING

- 1 tablespoon unsweetened cocoa powder
- 2 tablespoons granulated sugar
- 1 teaspoon cinnamon
- ¼ cup unsalted butter, melted
- 1 large egg, beaten

1. **For the Dough:** In a medium mixing bowl combine the 1 cup warm milk, 1 tablespoon sugar, and the yeast. Let stand 10 minutes. Add the 1 cup flour, ¾ cup milk, the salt, ¼ cup sugar, and the egg. Beat with a hand mixer until smooth. Stir in the melted butter. Set aside.

2. Place the 4 cups flour in the bowl of a stand mixer fitted with a dough hook. Add the 1 cup cold cut-up butter. Stir with a spoon to coat all of the butter pieces. Pour the yeast mixture into mixing bowl with flour. Blend with dough hook for 2 minutes to combine. Scrape sides. Blend 2 more minutes. Cover dough with plastic wrap and refrigerate at least 4 hours or overnight.

3. **For the Filling:** Meanwhile, stir together cocoa powder, sugar, and cinnamon. Line two large rimmed baking sheets with parchment paper; set aside. On a lightly floured surface, divide dough into four portions. Shape each portion into a ball. On floured surface, roll one of the balls into a 16-inch circle. Brush with some of the ¼ cup melted butter. Sprinkle with one-fourth of the cocoa mixture. Cut circle into eight wedges. Roll up wedges from long sides and place tip down on a prepared baking sheet. Repeat with remaining dough and filling. Let rise at room temperature 1 to 2 hours or until doubled in size.

4. Preheat oven to 375°F. Brush tops of croissants with beaten egg. Bake for 15 to 20 minutes or until browned.

IMPERIAL DEVIL'S FOOD BROWNIES

These decadent Death Star–shape brownies will keep local systems
in line—through sheer deliciousness, that is. If you're in a rush
to fend off attacking rebel forces, skip the decorating and cut
into 24 bars. You may fire up the oven when ready.

ACTIVE TIME 1 HR   TOTAL TIME 2 HRS 35 MIN   MAKES 24 STANDARD BROWNIES OR 8 DEATH STAR BROWNIES

BROWNIES

Nonstick cooking spray

¾ cup unsweetened cocoa powder

2 tablespoons instant coffee granules

½ teaspoon baking soda

⅔ cup unsalted butter, melted, divided

½ cup boiling water

2 cups granulated sugar

2 large eggs

1⅓ cups all-purpose flour

1 teaspoon vanilla extract

½ teaspoon kosher salt

GLAZE

1½ cups dark chocolate chips

6 tablespoons unsalted butter

2 tablespoons light corn syrup

½ teaspoon vanilla extract

DECORATION

Thin wooden skewers

Pastry tip

1 (1.5-ounce) can silver food color spray

1. **For the Brownies:** Heat oven to 350°F. Spray a 13×9-inch baking sheet with nonstick spray and line with parchment paper, extending the paper over the edges by 2 inches. Spray the parchment with nonstick spray; set aside.

2. In a large bowl whisk together cocoa, coffee granules, and baking soda. Stir in half of the melted butter. Add the boiling water and whisk until mixture thickens. Add sugar, eggs, and the remaining butter; whisk until smooth. Add flour, vanilla, and salt; whisk to blend completely.

3. Pour batter into prepared pan. Bake for 35 to 40 minutes or until brownies begin to pull away from sides of pan. Place pan on a rack and cool completely. Run a thin knife around edges of brownies. Lift brownies out by the parchment to a cutting board. Using a 3-inch round cookie cutter, cut the brownies into 8 circles and place on a rack over a baking sheet. (Save trimmings for another use or snacks.)

continued on page 98

continued from page 97

4. **For the Glaze:** In a microwave-safe bowl with a pour spout, combine chocolate chips, butter, and corn syrup. Heat the mixture in the microwave on high for 30 seconds. Stir and continue to heat at 30-second intervals until mixture is melted and smooth. Stir in vanilla.

5. Slowly pour the glaze over the brownie circles so they are completely covered. Let stand at room temperature until chocolate is completely set, about 1 hour, or refrigerate to speed things up.

6. **For the Decoration:** Working one at a time, place one skewer over the middle of the brownie. Insert the pointed end of the pastry tip just above the skewer and to the right. Press down gently on the pastry tip until it just cuts into the brownie; leave in place. (This creates the Concave Dish Composite Beam Superlaser of the Death Star.) Lightly spray the top of the brownie with the silver food coloring. Carefully remove pastry tip and skewer; repeat with remaining glazed brownies.

PROTON TORPEDOES

Unleash your cooking creativity with these cupcakes baked in sugar cones and turned into high-velocity treats. They'll never fail to hit the spot.

ACTIVE TIME 1 HR   **TOTAL TIME 1 HR 30 MIN**   **MAKES 6 TO 8 CONES**

6 to 8 large sugar ice cream cones

1 (9-ounce) box yellow cake mix + ingredients called for on box

16 ounces orange candy melts

16 ounces green candy melts

36 each orange and green mini candy-coated chocolates

1. Preheat oven to 350°F. Remove center of a 12-inch tube pan and cover pan with a double layer of heavy-duty foil. Use a skewer or paring knife to poke 6 to 8 small holes in the foil, 2 ½ inches apart. Gently place a cone in each hole, pushing it down until only about 1 inch of cone is showing. Place filled pan on a baking sheet; set aside.

2. Prepare cake mix according to package directions. Divide batter among cones, each with about 2 to 3 tablespoons batter. Bake, rotating pan halfway through, 18 to 20 minutes or until a toothpick inserted in cake centers comes out clean. Transfer pan to a wire rack to cool completely.

3. Meanwhile, line a baking sheet with waxed paper; set aside. Place candy melts in separate microwave-safe bowls. Melt the candy in the microwave for 30 seconds. Stir, and continue to melt candy at 30-second intervals until completely melted and smooth. Transfer melted candy to two separate 2-cup measures. Holding the cones by the open end, carefully dip the tips of 3 or 4 of the cones, three-quarters of the way up the sides, in the orange melted candy. Place on the waxed paper. Repeat with remaining cones in the green melted candy. Chill cones in refrigerator about 10 minutes or until firm.

4. Dip the tops of cones in opposite-color candy coating and sprinkle with the orange and green candies.

5. Transfer remaining candy coating to two decorator bags. Pipe lines on sides of cones and place a few candies on the lines. Chill to set.

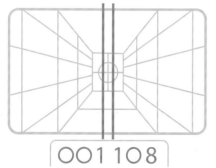

001108

CARBONITE CAKES

These honey-lemon-syrup-soaked pound cakes won't
last a fraction of the time that most things preserved in
carbonite do. Bake a batch and watch them disappear.

ACTIVE TIME 45 MIN   TOTAL TIME 1 HR 20 MIN   MAKES 7 CAKELETS

CAKELETS

Vegetable oil, for greasing
cake mold

1 ½ cups all-purpose flour, plus
more for dusting mold

¼ teaspoon baking powder

⅛ teaspoon baking soda

½ cup unsalted butter, room
temperature

1 cup granulated sugar

½ teaspoon vanilla extract

3 large eggs, room
temperature

½ cup lemon yogurt, room
temperature

2 tablespoons fresh
lemon juice

1 teaspoon finely grated
lemon zest

2 teaspoons black paste
food coloring

SYRUP

¼ cup honey

2 tablespoons fresh
lemon juice

¼ teaspoon gold luster dust

1. **For the Cakelets**: Heat oven to 325°F. Grease and flour *Star Wars* cakelet pan. Tap out excess flour.

2. In a medium bowl stir together flour, baking powder, and baking soda; set aside.

3. In a large mixing bowl beat butter with a hand mixer on medium speed for 30 seconds. Gradually add sugar, beating about 10 minutes or until light and fluffy. Beat in vanilla. Add eggs, one at a time, beating 1 minute after each addition and scraping bowl frequently.

4. With mixer on low speed, alternately add flour mixture and yogurt to butter mixture, beating well after each addition. Stir in lemon juice, lemon zest, and food coloring. Pour batter into mold, filling no more than two-thirds full.

5. Bake for 20 to 25 minutes or until a toothpick inserted in the center comes out mostly clean. Transfer mold to a rack and cool for 15 minutes. Tap pan firmly a few times, then invert and lift pan away. Turn cakelets face-side up.

6. **For the Syrup:** Meanwhile, combine honey and lemon juice in a small saucepan. Warm over medium-low heat, stirring to combine. Stir in luster dust. Gently brush warm syrup over the cakelets, allowing the syrup to absorb. Cool completely before serving.

NOTE: *Star Wars* Cakelet Pan is available at williams-sonoma.com.

TRASH COMPACTOR MONSTER COOKIES

These jumbo cookies mix together all kinds of things—oats, pretzels, chocolate chunks, oat cereal, and chewy candy bits. As they bake, you may hear Han Solo's infamous words, "What an incredible smell you've discovered!" (But only in a good way.) Be sure to keep these out of the hands of hungry creatures, like the dianoga.

ACTIVE TIME 30 MIN   TOTAL TIME 1 HR   MAKES 20 TO 24 JUMBO COOKIES

16 ounces peanut butter (do not use all-natural peanut butter)

½ cup butter, softened

½ cup brown sugar

½ cup granulated sugar

3 large eggs

1 teaspoon vanilla extract

4½ cups old-fashioned rolled oats

2 teaspoons baking soda

½ cup coarsely broken thin pretzel sticks or snaps

½ cup coarsely crushed wavy potato chips

½ cup semisweet chocolate chunks

½ cup circular oat cereal

½ cup snipped green soft candy (licorice, jelly beans, gummy rings, bears, or frogs)

1. Preheat oven to 350°F. Line two large rimmed baking sheets with parchment paper.

2. In the bowl of stand mixer fitted with the paddle attachment, combine peanut butter, butter, brown sugar, and granulated sugar. Mix until smooth.

3. Add eggs and vanilla; mix until combined. Add oats and baking soda; mix thoroughly.

4. Remove mixing bowl from the mixer. Gently fold in pretzels, chips, chocolate, cereal, and candy.

5. Using a ½ cup measure, portion out dough and gently shape into rough balls—don't press firmly or you will compact the dough too much. Place three cookie balls on a prepared baking sheet at a time so they have room to spread while baking. With moist hands, flatten slightly. Bake for 12 to 15 minutes or until edges are lightly browned. Remove from oven and cool on pan 5 minutes. Transfer cookies to a rack to cool completely. Repeat with remaining dough.

WHOLE-GRAIN FLATCAKES

When you can't make it to Canto Bight's casino buffet, enjoy these bubbly whole-grain breakfast breads at home, warm and slathered with butter and honey. Similar to an English muffin, they can also be split and toasted another morning.

ACTIVE TIME 45 MIN   TOTAL TIME 9 HRS 45 MIN   MAKES 15 FLATCAKES

2 cups bread flour

1 ½ cups whole wheat flour

1 envelope (2 ¼ teaspoons) instant dry yeast

2 tablespoons wheat germ

2 teaspoons granulated sugar

2 teaspoons kosher salt

1 ½ cups warm whole milk (120°F)

3 tablespoons butter, melted

1 large egg, beaten

Vegetable oil, for greasing bowl

Cornmeal

Butter and/or honey, for serving

1. In the bowl of a stand mixer fitted with a dough hook, combine bread flour, wheat flour, yeast, wheat germ, sugar, and salt. Stir until well combined. In another bowl whisk together milk, butter, and egg to combine. Add milk mixture to flour mixture. Mix with dough hook on medium-high speed until dough forms a ball and is elastic, about 15 minutes. Dough will be slightly sticky. Grease a large bowl with oil. Place dough in bowl and turn over to coat. Cover and refrigerate at least 8 hours or overnight.

2. Remove dough from refrigerator and let sit at room temperature for 1 hour.

3. Preheat oven to 350°F. Line two large rimmed baking sheets with parchment paper and sprinkle paper with cornmeal. On a lightly floured cutting board, divide dough into 15 equal pieces. Pinch and roll each piece into a ball. Place on prepared baking sheets. Sprinkle each ball with a little more cornmeal. Cover and let sit at room temperature for 45 minutes.

4. Heat a medium or large cast-iron skillet over low heat. Lightly flatten each ball to 1-inch thick. Place 3 or 4 dough balls in skillet and cook until bottom is golden, about 7 minutes. Flip and press dough down again. Cook another 5 to 7 minutes or until golden. Repeat with remaining dough.

5. Return flatcakes to prepared baking sheets and bake until cooked through, about 10 minutes.

6. Use a fork to split flatcakes. Serve warm with butter and/or honey.

DEX'S DINER PASTRY CASE

There's always a colorful crowd—and good food—at Dex's Diner in the CoCo Town neighborhood of Coruscant. With prepared puff pastry and just a few other ingredients, you'll be enjoying these flaky breakfast treats before you can say, "Jawa Juice!"

ICED DONUTS WITH SHREDDED COCONUT

MAKES 5 DONUTS AND HOLES

1. Preheat oven to 400°F. In a small bowl whisk together 1 egg yolk and 1 tablespoon water. Brush 1 thawed puff pastry sheet with egg wash; top with a second sheet and press together.

2. Using a 3-inch round cookie cutter, cut out five 3-inch rounds. Using a 1-inch round cookie cutter, cut out 1-inch holes from the centers. Bake the doughnuts (and holes) about 18 minutes or until golden brown; cool.

3. For the glaze, mix 1 cup powdered sugar with 1 to 2 tablespoons hot water until smooth; tint with food coloring, if desired. Dip the doughnuts in the glaze. Sprinkle with shredded coconut. Let stand until glaze sets.

MINI STICKY SWEETMALLOW BUNS

MAKES 20 MINI CINNAMON BUNS

1. Preheat oven to 350°F. Combine 1 cup brown sugar and 1 teaspoon cinnamon. Dust a work surface lightly with flour. Lightly roll out 1 thawed puff pastry sheet to a 9×10-inch rectangle. Brush with 1 tablespoon melted butter. Sprinkle with half of the brown sugar mixture. Starting on a short side, roll pastry up as tightly as you can. Use a sharp knife to cut the roll into ten 1-inch pieces. Place the rolls on a large parchment-lined baking sheet. Repeat with a second pastry sheet.

2. Bake 20 to 25 minutes or until puffed and golden brown.

3. Meanwhile, for the glaze, whisk together 1 cup powdered sugar, ½ teaspoon vanilla or maple extract, ¼ teaspoon salt, and 1 tablespoon whole milk.

4. Let rolls cool for 5 minutes, then drizzle with the glaze. Top with finely chopped pecans or walnuts, if you'd like.

WASAKA BERRY TURNOVERS

MAKES 8 TURNOVERS

1. Preheat oven to 350°F. In a small bowl whisk together 1 egg yolk and 1 tablespoon water to make an egg wash. Lightly dust a work surface with flour. Unfold 1 thawed sheet of puff pastry on the work surface Cut into four equal squares. Brush each square with 1 tablespoon melted butter.

2. Spoon 1 tablespoon raspberry jam or preserves in the center of each square. Brush edges of each square with egg wash. Fold one corner of each square over onto the opposite side to make a triangle. Gently press on the edges to seal. Transfer to a parchment-lined baking sheet.

3. Repeat with a second pastry sheet. Brush the tops of turnovers with egg wash and sprinkle with coarse sugar. Bake about 20 minutes or until golden brown. Let cool 5 to 10 minutes before serving.

SWAMP, VOLCANO & MINERAL WORLDS

From even the most inhospitable places—the swamps of Dagobah, lava-spewing mountains of Mustafar, and salt flats of Crait—comes a surprisingly tempting collection of treats, including a rich mud pie, wholesome bread rolls, and crunchy, chocolaty no-bake cookies.

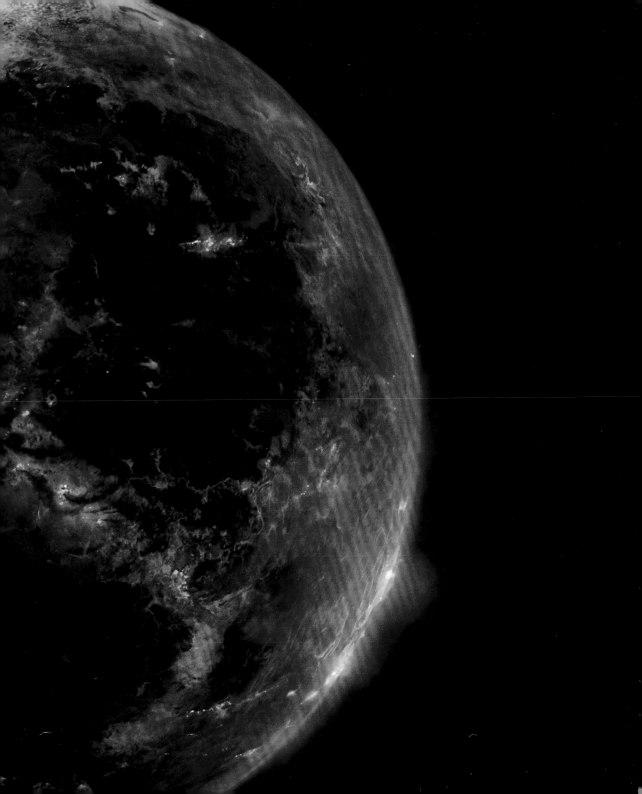

SWEET & SALTED CARAMEL CRAIT CUPCAKES

These Crait-inspired red-velvet cupcakes—topped with caramel–cream cheese frosting, a drizzle of caramel, and crunchy flaked salt—are so good that you may want to keep them hidden in your own secret base.

ACTIVE TIME 45 MIN   TOTAL TIME 1 HR 15   MAKES 24 CUPCAKES

CUPCAKES

- 1 (15.2-ounce) box red velvet cake mix + ingredients called for on package
- 1½ cups thick caramel topping, room temperature
- Large-grain flaked sea salt

FROSTING

- 1 cup unsalted butter, room temperature
- 4 ounces cream cheese, room temperature
- ⅓ cup thick caramel topping, room temperature
- 2 teaspoons vanilla extract
- ½ teaspoon kosher salt
- 4 cups powdered sugar

1. Preheat oven to 350°F. Place paper liners in two standard cupcake pans. Prepare red velvet cake mix as directed on package. Divide batter among liners and bake as directed. Cool cupcakes completely.

2. Meanwhile, prepare the frosting. Place butter and cream cheese in the bowl of a stand mixer fitted with a paddle attachment. Beat on medium speed until completely smooth, about 2 to 3 minutes. Add the ⅓ cup caramel topping, the vanilla, and kosher salt. Beat for another 2 minutes, scraping down the sides as needed. Reduce speed to low and add the powdered sugar a little at a time, beating until sugar is incorporated. Increase speed to medium, and beat until smooth and well-combined, about 2 to 3 minutes more.

3. Spread or pipe frosting on each cupcake, leaving a bit of the red velvet cupcake visible around the edges. Stir the 1½ cups caramel topping and, if necessary, warm in the microwave for 10 seconds to thin. With a spoon, drizzle each cupcake with about 1 tablespoon of the caramel, allowing it to cascade over the sides. Sprinkle each cupcake with a pinch or two of flaked salt.

MUSTAFARIAN MOLTEN LAVA CAKES

Make some fiery fun with these red velvet cakes that release
a delicious cream cheese filling when pierced with a spoon.
Serve them right out of the oven for maximum effect.

ACTIVE TIME 1 HR   TOTAL TIME 1 HR 15 MIN   MAKES 6 CAKES

FILLING

- 4 ounces cream cheese, room temperature
- 3 chocolate sandwich cookies
- 2 tablespoons granulated sugar
- 6 drops orange liquid food coloring
- 4 drops red liquid food coloring

CAKES

- Nonstick cooking spray
- 1½ cups granulated sugar, divided
- 1½ cups all-purpose flour
- 2 tablespoons unsweetened cocoa powder
- ½ teaspoon baking soda
- ¾ teaspoon kosher salt
- ¾ cup unsalted butter, melted
- ½ cup buttermilk
- 2 large egg yolks
- 1 (1-ounce) bottle red food coloring
- 2¼ teaspoons apple cider vinegar
- ¾ teaspoon vanilla extract

1. **For the Filling:** Line a small baking sheet with waxed paper. Place cream cheese in a small bowl. Separate sandwich cookies and with a knife; remove the white filling and add to the cream cheese. Reserve chocolate cookie halves—you will use them later. Add the sugar. Beat with a hand mixer on medium speed until completely blended. Beat in orange food coloring. Dot with six drops of red food coloring and pull through with a spoon to create a marble effect. Using an ice cream dipper, scoop filling into six rounds and place on the prepared baking sheet. Freeze about 1 hour or until firm.

2. **For the Cakes:** Preheat oven to 400°F. Spray six 8-ounce ramekins with nonstick spray. Sprinkle 2 tablespoons granulated sugar in each ramekin. Turn ramekin to coat entire interior, discarding excess sugar. Place on a large rimmed baking sheet and set aside.

continued on page 116

continued from page 115

3. Whisk together flour, cocoa, baking soda, and salt in a large mixing bowl. Add the remaining ½ cup sugar, the butter, buttermilk, egg yolks, red food coloring, vinegar, and vanilla. Mix thoroughly with a hand mixer until well blended, about 2 to 3 minutes.

4. Divide half of the batter evenly among ramekins. Remove frozen filling balls from freezer and place one in the center of each cake. Top with remaining batter, ensuring the filling is completely covered. Place a reserved cookie half on top of each cake and press very gently.

5. Bake cakes for 15 to 20 minutes or until the cakes are firm to the touch. Remove ramekins from oven and immediately run a thin knife around outer edge of cakes to loosen. Let stand for 5 minutes. Cover each ramekin with an inverted serving plate and carefully turn over. Lift off ramekin to unmold. Serve immediately.

SWAMP VINES

One bite of these crispy chocolate-butterscotch no-bake
treats, and you'll fight off a vine snake for another.

ACTIVE TIME 20 MIN   TOTAL TIME 30 MIN   MAKES 36 COOKIES

1 (12-ounce) bag semisweet
chocolate chips

1 (11-ounce) bag
butterscotch chips

6 ounces dark green candy
melts

1 (12-ounce) bag crispy
chow mein noodles

1 cup salted dry-roasted
peanuts

1 (3-ounce) container tiny
rainbow marshmallows

1. Line two large rimmed baking sheets with waxed paper or
parchment paper; set aside.

2. In a microwave-safe bowl combine the chocolate and
butterscotch chips. Heat in 30-second increments until
melted and smooth, stirring often. Set aside.

3. Place the green candy melts in a separate microwaveable
bowl. Heat and melt just as you did the chips. Stir until
smooth; set aside.

4. Place chow mein noodles in a large bowl. Moving quickly,
pour the melted chocolate and butterscotch chip mixture
over the noodles. Gently fold to thoroughly coat the noodles,
trying not to break them. Gently fold in the peanuts and
marshmallows—they should be completely coated.

5. Pour the green melted candy over the mixture and gently fold
one or two times to create green streaks throughout mixture.

6. Drop mixture by tablespoons onto prepared baking
sheets. Place in refrigerator for 10 to 15 minutes or until
chocolate is set.

YODA'S ROOTLEAF ROLLS

Dip these soft, fluffy rolls into a bowl of Rootleaf Stew. You can also
split, toast, and spread with Bantha butter and meiloorun jam for
breakfast, or use them as a vehicle for your favorite lunch meat
and cheese. These are perfect for Jedi in training!

ACTIVE TIME 45 MIN   TOTAL TIME 1 HR 15 MIN   MAKES 36 ROLLS

2 cups whole milk, warmed
to 105°F to 115°F

2 tablespoons honey

1 (0.25-ounce packet)
active dry yeast
(2¼ teaspoons)

3 tablespoons butter,
softened

4 medium carrots, peeled
and grated

1 teaspoon salt

4 ¾ cups all-purpose flour

⅓ cup unsalted roasted
sunflower seeds,
plus more for garnish
(optional)

1 egg, beaten with
1 tablespoon water

Dried dill and/or cumin
seeds (optional)

1. In a large bowl combine milk, honey, and yeast. Whisk until
well mixed. Let stand until a creamy foam begins to form,
about 5 minutes. Add butter and stir until melted. Add carrots
and salt; stir until combined.

2. Add flour, ½ cup at a time, to milk mixture, mixing until a soft
dough forms. Stir in the ⅓ cup sunflower seeds, mixing until
seeds are evenly distributed. Cover bowl with a clean, damp
kitchen towel.

3. Let dough rise about 30 minutes or until doubled in size.

4. Preheat oven to 450°F. Line two large rimmed baking sheets
with parchment paper. Divide dough into 36 equal pieces and
roll into balls. Arrange on prepared pans. Loosely cover with
clean towels or plastic wrap. Let rise 20 to 30 minutes or until
nearly doubled in size.

5. Brush the rolls with the egg wash, then sprinkle with
additional sunflower seeds, dried dill, and/or cumin
seeds, if using.

6. Bake 10 to 15 minutes or until lightly browned. Let cool slightly
on a wire rack before serving.

TO STORE: Store in an airtight container at room temperature
or freeze.

DAGOBAH BOG PIE

This deep, dark mud pie is swimming with good stuff—chocolate ice cream in a chocolate crust topped with sugar cookie "moss" and dark chocolate swamp vines. Yoda, Dagobah's most notable resident, was full of wise teachings, but his most astute may have been: "But now, we must eat. Come!"

ACTIVE TIME 45 MIN TOTAL TIME 3 HRS MAKES 1 (10-INCH) PIE (8 TO 10 SERVINGS)

PIE

Nonstick cooking spray

8 tablespoons unsalted butter, melted

1 (9-ounce) package thin chocolate wafers

1 quart chocolate ice cream

1 quart coffee ice cream

1 (16-ounce) jar thick hot fudge topping, room temperature

DECORATIONS

3 plain sugar cookies

1 teaspoon leaf green gel food coloring

1 cup semisweet chocolate chips

Chocolate jimmies

Gummy frogs (optional)

1. **For the Pie:** Preheat oven to 350°F. Spray a 10-inch springform pan with nonstick spray; set aside.

2. In a microwavable bowl melt butter. Place chocolate cookies in the bowl of a food processor fitted with a blade. Pulse a few times, then process until fine. Pour melted butter over the crumbs and pulse several times to combine. Remove ⅓ cup and set aside for topping. Transfer remaining mixture to prepared pan and press into the bottom of the pan using a flat-bottom measuring cup.

3. Bake 10 minutes. Remove from the oven and cool completely. Remove ice cream from freezer and soften at room temperature until spreadable. Carefully, evenly, and smoothly spread the chocolate ice cream over the crumb base using a spoon or offset spatula. Top with coffee ice cream. Press plastic wrap onto the surface and freeze about 1 hour or until firm.

4. When the ice cream has hardened, remove plastic wrap and quickly dollop with the chocolate fudge topping. With a large spoon, spread the topping over the ice cream—this does not have to be smooth. Sprinkle randomly with remaining chocolate crumbs, leaving a small border so the chocolate fudge peeks out. Cover the pan with foil and place in the freezer for at least 2 hours or overnight before serving.

continued on page 124

continued from page 123

5. **For the Decorations:** Place sugar cookies in the bowl of a food processor fitted with a blade. Pulse a few times, then process until fine. Dilute the food coloring in 2 teaspoons water. Add to food processor and pulse until green for the cookie "moss." Set aside.

6. Cover a small rimmed sheet pan with waxed paper. Place the chocolate chips in a small microwaveable bowl. Heat for 30 seconds, stir, and continue to heat at 30-second intervals until chocolate is melted and smooth. Place the chocolate in a small heavy-duty sealable plastic bag. Push the chocolate to a corner and twist the top like a pastry bag. Snip a tiny piece off the corner of the bag and pipe craggy sticklike shapes onto the waxed paper. Sprinkle with chocolate jimmies. Chill the chocolate shapes in the refrigerator about 20 minutes or until firm.

7. When ready to serve, remove the cake from the freezer and uncover. Release the outside ring of the pan and remove. Sprinkle the cookie moss randomly on top of the cake. Carefully peel the chocolate shapes from the waxed paper and place in the cookie toppings. Top with gummy frogs, if using.

8. Serve immediately, using a warm knife to slice.

INDEX

INSIGHT EDITIONS

PO Box 3088
San Rafael, CA 94912
www.insighteditions.com

Find us on Facebook: www.facebook.com/InsightEditions
Follow us on Twitter: @insighteditions

Disney • LUCASFILM

Library of Congress Cataloging-in-Publication Data available

ISBN 978-1-64722-377-9

INSIGHT EDITIONS
Publisher: Raoul Goff
VP of Licensing and Partnerships: Vanessa Lopez
VP of Creative: Chrissy Kwasnik
VP of Manufacturing: Alix Nicholaeff
Editorial Assistant: Harrison Tunggal
Managing Editor: Lauren LePera
Production Editor: Jennifer Bentham
Senior Production Manager: Greg Steffen
Senior Production Manager, Subsidiary Rights: Lina S. Palma

WATERBURY PUBLICATIONS, INC.
Editorial Director: Lisa Kingsley
Creative Director: Ken Carlson
Associate Editor: Tricia Bergman
Associate Art Director: Doug Samuelson
Photographer: Ken Carlson
Food Stylist: Jennifer Peterson
Food Stylist Assistant: Catherine Fitzpatrick

LUCASFILM
Senior Editor: Robert Simpson
Creative Director of Publishing: Michael Siglain
Art Director: Troy Alders
Asset Management: Bryce Pinkos, Chris Argyropoulos, Erik Sanchez, Gabrielle Levenson, Jason Schultz, Nicole LaCoursiere, Sarah Williams
Story Group: Emily Shkoukani, Kelsey Sharpe, Kate Izquierdo
Lucasfilm Art Department: Phil Szostak